dedicated to

marvin's garden

*which will bloom forever
in our hearts*

Bud

Round the Garden

written by Omri Glaser & illustrated by Byron Glaser & Sandra Higashi

Iris

HARRY N. ABRAMS, INC., PUBLISHERS

This is the tear

that made the puddle

that the sun evaporated

that made the cloud

cirrus

nimbostratus

cumulus

stratus

that made the rain fall

that watered the garden

extra fancy

POTATOES

XXX

that made the onion grow

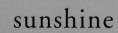

sunshine

carbon dioxide

rain

oxygen

soil

that made the gardeners cry.

Library of Congress Cataloging-in-Publication Data
Glaser, Omri.
Round the garden / written by Omri Glaser ;
illustrated by Byron Glaser and Sandra Higashi
p.   cm.
Summary: Traces the journey of a tear as it falls to the
ground, evaporates, reappears as rain, and waters a
garden to make an onion grow to produce more tears.
ISBN 0-8109-4137-6
[1. Hydrologic cycle Fiction. 2. Water Fiction. 3. Tears
Fiction. 4. Rain and rainfall Fiction.] I. Glaser, Byron, ill.
II. Higashi, Sandra, ill. III. Title.
PZ7.G48015Gar   2000
[E] – dc21   99–33289

Very special thanks to

EDWARD L. TRIPLETT, PHD.

of the Biochemistry Department at the
University of California, Santa Barbara,
for giving this book his blessing.

ARTISTS' NOTE

To create our artwork digitally, we first create rou
sketches on paper. Then, instead of transferring th
ideas to a traditional canvas, we transfer them to t
computer. We use the mouse just as we would a p
to further the visual concept into a more develope
illustration. On a traditional canvas, we would app
color by using brushes or cut-paper. On the comp
we do the same thing but use a digital palette. For
example, the colors we use are mixed just as they
be for a traditional painting. The artwork is then pr
on special paper.

Design by Sandra Higashi and Byron Glaser
Text copyright © 1999 Omri Glaser.
Illustrations copyright © 1999 Higashi Glaser Design

Printed and bound in Hong Kong

ABRAMS
HARRY N. ABRAMS, INC.
100 FIFTH AVENUE
NEW YORK, N.Y. 10011
www.abramsbooks.com